TAPPING INTO INTERNATIONAL NETWORKING 970
CHAPTER 4: THE ART OF CRAFTING A COMPELLING APPLICATION 971
  ACE THE VIRTUAL INTERVIEW 98
CHAPTER 5: NAVIGATING VISAS AND IMMIGRATION 99
  SEEKING LEGAL ASSISTANCE 100
CONCLUSION: YOUR JOURNEY TO A GLOBAL CAREER 101
INTRODUCTION 102
The Fundamentals of Passive Income 103
Building your passive income mindset 104
Exploring Real Estate Investments for Passive Income 105
Generating Passive Income through Dividend Investing 106
Creating Passive Income with Digital Products and Online Courses 107
Mastering affiliate marketing for passive income streams 87
Diversifying Your Passive Income Portfolio for Long-Term Success 90

INTRODUCTION

In today's rapidly evolving job market, job websites have become an invaluable tool for both job seekers and employers. With their user-friendly interfaces and vast databases, these platforms have revolutionized the way people find employment opportunities. This article delves into the world of job websites, shedding light on their significance, functionality, and benefits.

THE ROLE OF JOB WEBSITES IN MODERN JOB HUNTING

Job websites have emerged as the go-to solution for job seekers, offering a streamlined approach to finding employment. These platforms aggregate listings from various industries and present them in an organized manner. Whether you're a recent graduate, a seasoned professional looking for a career change, or someone re-entering the job market, these websites cater to everyone.

NAVIGATING THE INTERFACE: HOW JOB WEBSITES WORK

The simplicity of job websites is a significant draw. Users can easily browse through a plethora of job openings by filtering results based on their preferences. This includes factors like location, job type, experience level, and more. By utilizing these filters, individuals can pinpoint opportunities that align with their qualifications and aspirations, saving them time and effort.

CRAFTING AN IMPRESSIVE PROFILE

For job seekers, creating a compelling online profile is paramount. Job websites allow individuals to showcase their skills, experience, and accomplishments. It's essential to optimize your profile with relevant keywords that resonate with your desired job role. This optimization ensures that your profile appears in relevant employer searches, increasing your visibility.

THE POWER OF NOTIFICATIONS

Many job websites offer a feature that sends alerts to users when new job listings matching their criteria are posted. This feature is a game-changer, as it keeps job seekers informed in real-time. By setting up these notifications, you can stay ahead of the competition and promptly apply to fresh job opportunities.

BENEFITS FOR EMPLOYERS

Job websites are not only beneficial for job seekers but also for employers aiming to find suitable candidates. These platforms provide a cost-effective solution for recruitment. Employers can post job openings, specify job requirements, and browse through a pool of potential candidates. This targeted approach saves time and resources in the hiring process.

TRANSITIONING TO A NEW CAREER PATH

For individuals looking to transition into a new career, job websites offer a seamless way to explore alternative options. Whether you're switching industries or pursuing a passion, these platforms connect you with opportunities that might have otherwise gone unnoticed.

SUPPORTING THE JOB MARKET

In the ever-evolving landscape of employment, job websites play a crucial role in bridging the gap between job seekers and employers. Their user-friendly interfaces, advanced search capabilities, and real-time updates have redefined the job hunting process. As technology continues to advance, these platforms are likely to become even more sophisticated, providing an increasingly personalized experience.

UPWORK: THE GATEWAY TO GLOBAL OPPORTUNITIES

In rapidly evolving work landscape, the traditional 9-to-5 job is giving way to flexible and dynamic opportunities. Enter Upwork, the platform that has redefined how freelancers connect with clients worldwide. Upwork serves as a gateway to a plethora of global opportunities, enabling freelancers to showcase their skills and expertise on an international stage.

Upwork's unparalleled reach allows freelancers to tap into a diverse array of projects spanning various industries and sectors. From web development and graphic design to content creation and digital marketing, the platform caters to a wide range of skills. This diverse project pool empowers freelancers to explore their passions, diversify their portfolio, and continuously evolve their professional journey.

One of Upwork's standout features is its capacity to facilitate remote work arrangements. As geographical barriers fade away, freelancers can collaborate with clients from different corners of the world without the constraints of location. This flexibility not only broadens freelancers' horizons but also offers clients access to a global talent pool, ensuring they find the perfect match for their projects.

Creating a compelling profile on Upwork is essential for freelancers to attract high-paying clients. A well-crafted profile highlights skills, showcases past work, and communicates the freelancer's unique value proposition. Through a combination of a captivating bio, portfolio samples, and client testimonials, freelancers can establish credibility and differentiate themselves in a competitive landscape.

To optimize success on Upwork, freelancers can follow a few key strategies:

- Craft an Engaging Profile: Describe your skills concisely and showcase relevant experience to demonstrate your expertise.
- Highlight Niche Specialization: Specializing in a specific niche can help you stand out and attract clients seeking specialized skills.
- Pricing Strategy: Set competitive rates that reflect your skill level and experience while remaining attractive to potential clients.
- Regularly Update Portfolio: Showcase your latest and best work to give clients a comprehensive view of your capabilities.
- Responsive Communication: Timely and clear communication fosters trust with clients and helps build long-lasting relationships.

Embrace the Upwork platform to embark on a journey that transcends geographical boundaries and embraces the global nature of work. Whether you're a seasoned freelancer or just starting, Upwork offers the resources and opportunities to thrive in today's interconnected world. Join Upwork today and unleash your potential on the global stage.

DESIGNHILL: WHERE CREATIVITY MEETS COMMERCE

Step into the realm of boundless creativity with Designhill, your ultimate destination for unleashing your artistic potential. This platform is tailor-made for designers, offering a captivating space to explore the realms of logos, graphics, and branding projects while equipping you with the strategies to showcase your skills with impact.

Designhill serves as a thriving ecosystem where creative from around the world converge to transform ideas into visual masterpieces. Dive headfirst into a spectrum of projects that encompass logo design, graphic artistry, and the art of branding. This dynamic environment not only allows you to stretch your creative muscles but also provides a springboard to turn your passion into a lucrative venture.

At the core of Designhill lies the fusion of art and commerce. As a designer, you have the opportunity to craft compelling visual identities that resonate with clients and their audiences. Whether it's a startup seeking an eye-catching logo or an established brand in need of a fresh rebrand, Designhill's projects provide a canvas to translate concepts into captivating visuals.

But it's not just about the artwork. Designhill equips you with the strategies to effectively showcase your skills and make your mark in a competitive landscape. Craft a profile that speaks volumes about your expertise, showcase a portfolio that illustrates your versatility, and engage with clients in a way that fosters collaboration and trust.

Here's how to make the most of your Designhill experience:

- Craft a Captivating Profile: Let your profile reflect your unique style and expertise, making an impactful first impression on potential clients.
- Build a Versatile Portfolio: Showcase a diverse range of your best work to demonstrate your ability to tackle various design challenges.
- Interact and Collaborate: Effective communication and collaboration with clients enhance your reputation and foster lasting relationships.
- Stay Updated: Keep your skills current and adapt to design trends to maintain a competitive edge in the ever-evolving design landscape.

Designhill is more than a platform; it's a community that empowers designers to thrive creatively and commercially. With each project you take on, you're not just crafting visuals; you're shaping brands, telling stories, and contributing to the visual language of our interconnected world.

Step onto Designhill's stage, where creativity and commerce coalesce to inspire, challenge, and reward your design journey. Uncover your potential today, and let your creativity take center stage on the global design arena.

TOPTAL: ELEVATING ELITE FREELANCERS

Embark on a journey of excellence with Toptal, the platform that curates an exclusive network of top-tier freelancers and connects them with discerning elite clients. Discover the world of unparalleled opportunities, where expertise is paramount and quality is the hallmark of every project. Dive into Toptal's meticulous screening process and grasp the strategies to position yourself as a true expert in your field.

Toptal stands as a beacon for freelancers who have honed their skills to perfection. It caters to clients who demand nothing but the best, making it the go-to platform for those seeking exceptional talent. By joining Toptal's elite network, you gain access to projects that are not only intellectually stimulating but also financially rewarding.

At the heart of Toptal's reputation lies its stringent screening process. The platform handpicks freelancers who demonstrate exceptional proficiency and a proven track record. This process ensures that every member of the network embodies the highest standards of skill and professionalism. As a Toptal freelancer, you become part of an exclusive community that shares a commitment to excellence.

Positioning yourself as an expert on Toptal requires a strategic approach:

- Showcase Your Expertise: Highlight your specialized skills, backed by a portfolio that reflects your mastery of your craft.
- Craft a Compelling Profile: Craft a profile that concisely communicates your capabilities and showcases your accomplishments.
- Emphasize Quality: Prioritize quality over quantity, delivering exceptional work that aligns with Toptal's reputation.

- **Build Strong Client Relationships:** Cultivate strong client relationships by demonstrating professionalism, effective communication, and reliability.
- **Stay Current:** Continuously update your skills to stay at the forefront of your field, demonstrating your commitment to growth and innovation.

Toptal's ethos revolves around excellence, and as a part of this network, you have the opportunity to work with like-minded peers and esteemed clients who share your dedication to exceptional outcomes. Elevate your freelancing career to new heights by joining Toptal's exclusive platform where elite freelancers flourish and where your expertise is celebrated and rewarded.

LINKEDIN AND LINKEDIN SERVICES MARKETPLACE: THE POWER OF PROFESSIONAL NETWORKING

Unlock the potential of professional networking with LinkedIn, a platform that empowers you to cultivate a robust online presence and naturally draw in clients. Delve into the world of connections and collaborations, while also uncovering the valuable resource of the LinkedIn Services Marketplace—a hidden gem designed for specialized freelancers.

LinkedIn, often dubbed the professional's social network, offers a unique platform to showcase your skills, experience, and expertise. It goes beyond the traditional social media landscape, providing a space where you can connect with industry peers, potential clients, and partners. By crafting a compelling profile that highlights your accomplishments and resonates with your target audience, you can attract clients organically.

The power of LinkedIn lies in its ability to facilitate meaningful connections. Through engaging content, insightful articles, and active participation in relevant groups, you can position yourself as a thought leader in your field. This not only boosts your visibility but also builds trust among your network, gradually leading to potential collaborations and projects.

However, the hidden treasure within LinkedIn's ecosystem is the LinkedIn Services Marketplace. This feature offers specialized freelancers a dedicated platform to showcase their skills and services directly to a receptive audience. Clients seeking specific expertise can easily discover freelancers with the right qualifications, making it a valuable resource for both parties.

Here's how you can leverage LinkedIn and the Services Marketplace:

- Optimize Your Profile: Craft a detailed profile that outlines your skills, experience, and achievements, making a lasting impression on potential clients.
- Share Valuable Content: Regularly share industry insights, tips, and trends to establish yourself as an authority in your field.
- Network Strategically: Connect with professionals who align with your industry and goals, fostering meaningful relationships.
- Engage Actively: Participate in discussions, comment on relevant posts, and share your perspective to engage your network.

- Explore the Services Marketplace: Create a compelling listing in the Services Marketplace to showcase your specialized skills and attract clients seeking your expertise.

LinkedIn offers an unparalleled platform for professionals to connect, collaborate, and grow. It's not just a place to find jobs; it's a hub for building relationships, nurturing your personal brand, and accessing a pool of potential clients. Tap into the power of LinkedIn and its Services Marketplace to transform your freelancing career and seize the opportunities that await within your professional network.

WE WORK REMOTELY: EMBRACING REMOTE WORK CULTURE

Step into the future of work with We Work Remotely, a platform that invites you to fully embrace the remote work revolution. Navigate the intricacies of remote work culture, refine your skills in creating remote-friendly proposals, and discover projects that align perfectly with your expertise.

We Work Remotely is more than just a platform; it's a gateway to a world where geography knows no bounds. As the global workforce shifts towards remote arrangements, this platform empowers you to leverage your skills from the comfort of your chosen workspace, regardless of physical location.

Crafting remote-friendly proposals is an art that We Work Remotely helps you master. Tailor your proposals to showcase your ability to excel in remote collaborations. Highlight your communication skills, time management, and self-discipline – qualities that are instrumental in the success of remote work dynamics. By doing so, you'll stand out and resonate with clients seeking professionals who can seamlessly contribute to projects from a distance.

Here's how you can make the most of We Work Remotely:

- Polish Your Remote Profile: Create a profile that emphasizes your experience with remote work and your capacity to thrive in a virtual environment.
- Refine Proposal Techniques: Craft proposals that not only demonstrate your expertise but also underscore your suitability for remote collaboration.
- Showcase Remote Skills: Highlight skills like effective virtual communication, self-motivation, and adaptability to excel in remote projects.
- Research Companies: Explore the companies posting remote jobs and projects, ensuring they align with your skills and aspirations.
- Remote Networking: Engage with other remote professionals to exchange insights, strategies, and experiences, fostering a thriving remote work community.

We Work Remotely offers a multitude of projects and opportunities that cater to a diverse range of skills. From programming and design to marketing and customer support, the platform spans various industries, ensuring that you can find projects that resonate with your passion and expertise.

As the world continues to embrace remote work, We Work Remotely positions you at the forefront of this transformative movement. Embrace the flexibility, autonomy, and global connectivity that remote work offers. Explore We Work Remotely to discover projects that not only complement your skills but also empower you to flourish in the evolving landscape of work.

BEHANCE: SHOWCASING YOUR CREATIVE PORTFOLIO

Elevate your creative journey with Behance, the platform that transforms into your virtual portfolio, allowing you to showcase your creative projects to a global audience. Discover how to curate an impressive profile that captures attention and effortlessly converts views into potential clients.

Behance is a haven for creators seeking to exhibit their artistic prowess. As an online gallery of creative works, it enables you to present your projects, whether they're designs, illustrations, photography, or any other form of artistic expression. The platform's global reach ensures that your creations transcend geographical boundaries, reaching fellow creative, clients, and enthusiasts around the world.

Your Behance profile is your digital canvas, where you can craft a narrative that tells the story of your creative journey. By effectively showcasing your best work, you not only attract attention but also establish your unique artistic identity. Each project you share becomes a window into your skills, process, and aesthetic, giving potential clients a glimpse into what you can offer.

Here's how to maximize your Behance experience:

- Curate a Captivating Portfolio: Choose a selection of your finest work that demonstrates your range and expertise within your creative niche.
- Craft a Compelling Profile: Write a bio that succinctly captures your creative philosophy, experience, and aspirations.

- Share Insightful Descriptions: Accompany your projects with descriptions that provide context, explaining your thought process and the story behind each creation.
- Engage with the Community: Interact with fellow creative by appreciating their work, offering feedback, and participating in discussions.
- Convert Views into Clients: Make it easy for potential clients to reach out by including contact information or directing them to your website or portfolio.

Behance serves not only as a platform for self-expression but also as a stepping stone toward professional growth. It's a space where your passion meets potential, where your creations resonate with kindred spirits, and where clients discover your unique talent. By mastering the art of presenting your work on Behance, you can transform casual viewers into enthusiastic patrons of your creative endeavors.

SIMPLYHIRED: SIMPLICITY IN JOB HUNTING

Experience the ease of job hunting with SimplyHired, the platform that cuts through the noise and clutter to provide a user-friendly experience. Uncover the secrets to effortlessly finding freelancing gigs that perfectly match your skills and preferences, all within a streamlined platform.

In a world saturated with job search platforms, SimplyHired stands out by living up to its name – simplicity. Navigating through the platform is a breeze, thanks to its intuitive design and straightforward interface. This user-friendly approach ensures that your job search is focused and efficient, allowing you to save time and energy while finding the perfect freelancing opportunities.

SimplyHired is more than just a job search engine; it's a strategic tool that empowers you to tailor your search to your unique skills and preferences. Whether you're a seasoned freelancer or just starting your journey, the platform offers a range of options that span different industries, skill sets, and project types.

Here's how to master the art of finding freelancing gigs on SimplyHired:

- Refine Your Search: Utilize filters and search options to narrow down listings based on your skills, location, and other preferences.
- Create Custom Alerts: Set up job alerts to receive notifications about new gigs that align with your criteria.

- **Explore Detailed Listings:** Dive into comprehensive job listings that provide clear descriptions, requirements, and expectations.
- **Optimize Your Profile:** Craft a concise yet compelling profile that showcases your skills and experience, making you stand out to potential clients.
- **Apply Strategically:** Tailor your applications to each job, emphasizing how your skills match the project's needs.

SimplyHired commitment to simplicity ensures that you can focus on what truly matters: finding freelancing gigs that resonate with your expertise and aspirations. Say goodbye to overwhelming searches and hello to a hassle-free journey toward your next freelancing endeavor.

DRIBBBLE: THE DESIGNER'S PARADISE

Embark on a creative journey like no other with Dribbble, the platform that offers designers a paradise to showcase their talents. Unearth the strategies that will elevate you in a competitive landscape, helping you secure projects that align perfectly with your design aesthetic.

Dribbble isn't just a platform; it's a vibrant community that celebrates creativity in its purest form. Designers from around the globe come together here to share their work, exchange ideas, and inspire one another. It's a space where your design journey is nurtured, celebrated, and elevated to new heights.

In a field as competitive as design, standing out is essential. Dribbble provides you with the canvas to display your portfolio and demonstrate your skills. By curating your best work, you not only attract attention but also set the stage to secure projects that resonate with your design style.

Here's how you can excel on Dribbble:

- Create a Striking Portfolio: Showcase a diverse range of projects that highlight your versatility and mastery in various design disciplines.
- Craft an Impactful Profile: Your bio should succinctly convey your design philosophy and the unique perspective you bring to your projects.
- Engage Actively: Interact with fellow designers by appreciating their work, participating in discussions, and fostering a sense of community.
- Consistency is Key: Regularly update your profile with your latest and best work to keep your portfolio fresh and relevant.
- Showcase Your Process: Share insights into your design process, providing a glimpse into how you transform ideas into visually captivating creations.

Dribbble is a haven for designers seeking inspiration, connection, and opportunity. By sharing your designs on this platform, you not only share your creations but also open doors to collaborations, freelance projects, and potential clients who are drawn to your distinct style.

In a world where design is a language that transcends boundaries, Dribbble offers you a stage to amplify your voice and leave a mark.

Immerse yourself in the world of design. Immerse yourself in Dribbble.

FIVERR: YOUR MICRO-ENTREPRENEURSHIP JOURNEY

Embark on a micro-entrepreneurial adventure with Fiverr, the platform that empowers you to offer specialized services and build a unique venture. Discover the strategies to set your prices strategically and optimize your gigs for success.

Fiverr isn't just a marketplace; it's a gateway to your micro-entrepreneurship journey. Whether you're a designer, writer, developer, or possess any other skill, Fiverr offers you a platform to turn your expertise into a thriving business. It's a space where you can offer your services, connect with clients worldwide, and cultivate a niche micro-business that aligns with your passions.

The art of success on Fiverr involves more than just listing your skills. It's about crafting compelling gigs that resonate with potential clients and showcasing your value in a competitive market. Setting your prices appropriately is a critical aspect of this journey. By striking a balance between competitive rates and the value you provide, you position yourself as a micro-entrepreneur who offers quality and expertise.

Here's how you can excel on Fiverr:

- Define Your Niche: Identify your unique skill set and carve a niche that differentiates you from the competition.

- Craft Attention-Grabbing Gigs: Create gig titles, descriptions, and images that not only inform but also captivate potential clients.
- Set Competitive Prices: Research the market to determine fair and competitive rates that reflect your expertise.
- Build a Strong Portfolio: Showcase your best work to demonstrate your capabilities and build client confidence.
- Prioritize Communication: Maintain clear and responsive communication with clients to foster trust and long-lasting relationships.

Fiverr is your platform to flex your entrepreneurial muscles on a micro scale. It's where your expertise, combined with strategic pricing and optimized gigs, transforms into a compelling micro-entrepreneurship venture. Your journey on Fiverr isn't just about offering services; it's about building a brand, cultivating client relationships, and growing a business that reflects your unique skills and passions.

PEOPLEPERHOUR: HOURLY PROJECTS, LIFETIME OPPORTUNITIES

Embark on a journey of hourly projects and boundless opportunities with PeoplePerHour. Explore the platform's versatile offerings for both short-term tasks and long-term collaborations. Uncover strategies to manage your time effectively while consistently delivering exceptional results.

PeoplePerHour is more than just a platform; it's a dynamic hub for freelancers seeking both short-term gigs and enduring partnerships. From quick tasks to extensive projects, the platform's diverse range of opportunities caters to a variety of skills and industries.

Efficiency is key when working on hourly projects, and PeoplePerHour empowers you to manage your time effectively without compromising on quality. By honing your time management skills, you can seamlessly balance multiple tasks and maintain a reputation for delivering top-notch results on schedule.

Here's how you can excel on PeoplePerHour:

- Curate Your Profile: Create a profile that showcases your expertise, experience, and specialization to attract relevant projects.
- Set Realistic Hourly Rates: Determine rates that reflect your skills, experience, and the market's expectations.
- Communicate Clearly: Establish clear communication channels with clients to ensure mutual understanding and avoid misunderstandings.
- Embrace Time Management: Prioritize tasks, set milestones, and allocate time effectively to meet project deadlines.
- Deliver Consistently: Maintain a high standard of work to establish a reputation for reliability and excellence.

PeoplePerHour provides the flexibility to work on projects that align with your skill set and preferences while offering the chance to build lasting relationships with clients seeking ongoing support. As you navigate through hourly projects and engage in collaborations, you're not just managing time; you're crafting opportunities that can shape your freelancing journey.

GURU: WHERE FREELANCERS AND EMPLOYERS UNITE

Discover the synergy between freelancers and employers on Guru, the platform that bridges the gap and offers a diverse spectrum of projects. Dive into the world of opportunities, connect with employers who value your expertise, and master the art of crafting winning proposals and negotiating contracts like a seasoned professional.

Guru isn't just a platform; it's a dynamic marketplace where freelancers and employers converge to collaborate and create. With a vast array of projects spanning various domains, Guru ensures that freelancers of all specialties can find opportunities that align with their skills and passions.

Crafting a winning proposal is a skill that Guru helps you refine. It's about more than just your expertise; it's about presenting your value proposition in a way that resonates with potential clients. By showcasing your capabilities, understanding the project requirements, and aligning your proposal with the client's needs, you can stand out and demonstrate your commitment to delivering exceptional results.

Here's how you can thrive on Guru:

- Create a Compelling Profile: Craft a profile that succinctly captures your skills, experience, and the unique perspective you bring to your projects.
- Tailor Your Proposals: Customize your proposals to demonstrate your understanding of the project and how you're the ideal fit for the task.
- Negotiate Professionally: Engage in negotiations that reflect your value while remaining flexible to reach mutually beneficial terms.
- Showcase Your Portfolio: Highlight your best work to illustrate your capabilities and showcase your track record of success.
- Deliver Quality: Consistently deliver high-quality work to build a strong reputation and foster long-lasting client relationships.

Guru provides a platform where freelancers and employers converge, creating a thriving ecosystem of collaboration and innovation. As you navigate through projects, proposals, and contracts, you're not just building your freelancing career; you're building connections, reputation, and a portfolio of accomplishments.

FREELANCER.COM: YOUR ONE-STOP FREELANCING HUB

Embark on a journey of boundless opportunities with Freelancer.com, your ultimate destination for freelancing endeavors. Discover the breadth of projects available and uncover the strategies to maximize your earnings. Learn how to master bidding techniques and cultivate a loyal client base for sustained success.

Freelancer.com isn't just a platform; it's a bustling hub where freelancers connect with clients seeking a myriad of skills and services. From creative tasks to technical projects, the platform offers a comprehensive range of opportunities that cater to your expertise.

Maximizing your earnings on Freelancer.com requires a strategic approach to bidding. It's not about simply quoting a price; it's about presenting a tailored proposal that showcases your understanding of the project, your skills, and the value you bring. By mastering the art of effective bidding, you can stand out in a competitive landscape and secure projects that align with your capabilities.

Here's how you can excel on Freelancer.com:

Optimize Your Profile: Create a detailed profile that highlights your skills, experience, and the unique value you offer.

Research and Target: Thoroughly research projects before bidding, ensuring they align with your skills and preferences.

Craft Winning Proposals: Tailor your proposals to address the project's specific requirements and showcase your expertise.

Set Competitive Rates: Determine rates that reflect your skills and market trends while remaining attractive to potential clients.

Deliver Quality Work: Consistently provide high-quality work to build a strong reputation and secure repeat clients.

Freelancer.com serves as a dynamic arena where freelancers and clients converge to create meaningful collaborations. As you navigate through projects, bids, and successful contracts, you're not just freelancing; you're building relationships, honing your skills, and establishing a presence in the freelancing community.

DESIGNCROWD: CROWD-POWERED DESIGN EXCELLENCE

Unlock the boundless creativity of the crowd with DesignCrowd, the platform that harnesses collective talent to achieve design excellence. Dive into the world of design contests and learn how to leverage your skills to not only excel but also win projects that showcase your creative prowess.

DesignCrowd is more than just a platform; it's a dynamic arena where designers, clients, and creativity converge. Through design contests, you have the opportunity to showcase your skills by submitting your best work based on client briefs. The platform's crowd-powered approach ensures that you're not just competing against others, but collaborating with a diverse pool of creative minds to achieve outstanding results.

Excelling in design contests on DesignCrowd requires a strategic approach. It's about understanding the client's vision, infusing your unique flair, and delivering designs that stand out in a competitive field. By mastering this art, you can not only receive recognition for your creativity but also secure projects that reflect your expertise.

Here's how you can thrive on DesignCrowd:

- Create Captivating Designs: Craft designs that capture the essence of the client's brief while infusing your distinctive style.
- Study the Brief: Understand the client's requirements, preferences, and objectives to create designs that resonate.
- Incorporate Feedback: Embrace feedback and iterate on your designs to meet the client's vision and expectations.
- Engage with the Community: Connect with fellow designers, share insights, and learn from others' experiences.
- Build a Strong Portfolio: Showcase your successful contest entries to attract potential clients seeking your creative expertise.

DesignCrowd's unique platform taps into the collaborative power of designers worldwide. As you engage in design contests and collaborate with the crowd, you're not just competing; you're contributing to a global creative conversation, honing your skills, and leaving a lasting imprint on design projects.

WELLFOUND: NAVIGATING NEW OPPORTUNITIES

Embark on a journey of new opportunities with Wellfound, the platform tailored for specialized projects in design and development. Discover how to effectively present your expertise, stand out in a competitive landscape, and secure valuable gigs that align with your skills.

Wellfound isn't just another platform; it's a niche hub where designers and developers find projects that resonate with their unique talents. Focused exclusively on design and development, Wellfound offers a curated space that connects freelancers with clients seeking specialized skills and innovative solutions.

Standing out on Wellfound requires more than just listing your skills; it's about crafting a compelling profile that showcases your expertise concisely and effectively. By presenting your capabilities in a way that resonates with potential clients, you increase your chances of being noticed and considered for projects that align with your strengths.

Here's how you can navigate Wellfound with success:

Create a Tailored Profile: Craft a profile that highlights your specialized skills, experience, and accomplishments in design and development.

Curate Your Portfolio: Showcase projects that demonstrate your expertise and showcase your ability to tackle complex design and development challenges.

Embrace Clarity: Clearly communicate your value proposition, describing how your skills can address clients' unique needs.

Engage Actively: Participate in discussions, connect with other professionals, and foster a sense of community on the platform.

Deliver Excellence: Consistently provide high-quality work that aligns with the caliber of projects you seek on Wellfound.

Wellfound provides a space where designers and developers can explore opportunities that challenge and inspire their skills. As you navigate through projects, engage with clients, and collaborate with fellow professionals, you're not just freelancing; you're building a reputation, contributing to a specialized community, and forging a path to excellence.

99DESIGNS: DESIGNING YOUR SUCCESS STORY

Unlock the secrets of 99designs, a platform that holds the key to freelancers' success stories in the world of design. From logo design to web projects, delve into a realm of creative opportunities that allow you to elevate your design game and leave your mark in the competitive landscape.

99designs isn't just a platform; it's a creative playground where designers can showcase their talents and bring visions to life. With projects spanning various design disciplines, from logos to websites, the platform provides a canvas for you to flex your creative muscles and demonstrate your unique style.

Designing your success story on 99designs involves more than just creating visuals; it's about understanding clients' needs, infusing creativity, and delivering designs that captivate and resonate. By mastering this art, you can stand out in the crowded design space and showcase your expertise to a global audience.

Here's how you can excel on 99designs:

- Create Impactful Designs: Craft designs that not only meet clients' briefs but also showcase your creativity and artistic flair.
- Understand the Vision: Grasp the essence of clients' ideas and translate them into compelling visual narratives.
- Engage in Collaboration: Embrace client feedback and collaborate effectively to refine and enhance your designs.
- Build a Strong Portfolio: Showcase your best designs to create a compelling showcase of your skills and capabilities.
- Stay Ahead of Trends: Keep your design skills and knowledge current to remain at the forefront of design trends.

99designs offers a platform where designers can transform their creativity into tangible success stories. As you navigate through diverse projects, collaborate with clients, and share your designs with the world, you're not just designing; you're crafting your narrative and contributing to the ever-evolving landscape of design.

WORKING NOT WORKING: WHERE CREATIVE MINDS THRIVE

Enter a world where creative minds flourish — welcome to Working Not Working. This platform is a haven for those who seek to thrive in the realm of creativity. Whether you're a designer, writer, illustrator, or any kind of creative professional, Working Not Working is designed to cater to your unique talents and aspirations.

Working Not Working isn't just a platform; it's a community that celebrates the art of creativity. It brings together top-tier creative talents and visionary companies in a space where connections are formed, collaborations are born, and groundbreaking projects come to life.

On Working Not Working, you'll discover a space that values quality over quantity. The platform focuses on bringing together top-notch creatives with companies that understand the true value of originality and innovation. If you're a creative seeking a platform that recognizes your worth and provides you with opportunities that resonate, Working Not Working is the place to be.

This is where the freelance gig isn't just a transaction – it's an artistic partnership. It's where your skills, passion, and vision find a home. As you navigate through projects, engage with clients, and connect with fellow creative, you're not just working; you're thriving, creating, and making your mark on the world of creativity.

WEBFLOW EXPERTS: MASTERING THE WEBFLOW PLATFORM

Unlock the potential of Webflow Experts to secure web design and development projects that elevate your career. Position yourself as a Webflow specialist and attract clients who are seeking cutting-edge websites that seamlessly combine design and functionality.

Webflow Experts isn't just a platform; it's a gateway to becoming a master of the Webflow platform – a space where your web design and development skills can truly shine. As a Webflow specialist, you can leverage the platform's unique capabilities to create stunning, interactive, and responsive websites that push the boundaries of design and technology.

Positioning yourself as a Webflow specialist involves more than just technical expertise; it about understands the nuances of the platform and its potential for innovation. By showcasing your proficiency in Webflow, you can attract clients who recognize the value of having a modern, dynamic, and user-friendly website that stands out in a crowded digital landscape.

Here's how you can excel as a Webflow Expert:

- Showcase Your Portfolio: Create a portfolio that highlights your successful Webflow projects, demonstrating your design and development skills.
- Highlight Your Expertise: Emphasize your proficiency in leveraging Webflow's features to create visually appealing and functional websites.

- Position Your Brand: Craft a profile that positions you as a specialist in Webflow, emphasizing your unique skills and experiences.
- Engage with the Community: Connect with fellow Webflow Experts, share insights, and stay updated on the latest trends and developments.
- Deliver Excellence: Consistently provide high-quality work that aligns with the standards of Webflow's innovative platform.

Webflow Experts offers a platform where your web design and development talents can flourish. As you navigate through projects, collaborate with clients, and engage with the Webflow community, you're not just building websites; you're shaping digital experiences, pushing the boundaries of design, and leaving your mark on the online world.

YUNOJUNO: SIMPLIFYING FREELANCER-CLIENT CONNECTIONS

Dive into the world of streamlined freelancer-client interactions with YunoJuno. Uncover the seamless experience of managing projects, contracts, and payments all within one user-friendly interface.

YunoJuno isn't just another platform; it's a solution that redefines the way freelancers and clients collaborate. With a focus on simplicity and efficiency, YunoJuno eliminates the complexities often associated with project management, allowing you to focus on what you do best – delivering exceptional work.

The platform's user-friendly interface brings together freelancers and clients, facilitating seamless communication, project tracking, and contract management. From negotiating terms to ensuring timely payments, YunoJuno streamlines every step of the freelancing process.

Here's how YunoJuno simplifies your freelancing experience:

- Effortless Project Management: Manage projects with ease, keeping track of tasks, timelines, and milestones within a single platform.
- Streamlined Contracts: Generate, sign, and manage contracts digitally, ensuring clarity and transparency throughout the engagement.
- Secure Payments: Enjoy hassle-free payments with built-in invoicing and payment processing, eliminating the need for external tools.
- Clear Communication: Communicate seamlessly with clients, ensuring everyone is on the same page and expectations are met.
- Centralized Workspace: Access all project-related information in one place, reducing the need for multiple tools and platforms.

YunoJuno's innovative approach simplifies the freelancer-client relationship, enabling you to focus on delivering your expertise without the administrative headaches. As you navigate through projects, collaborate with clients, and manage your freelance business, you're not just working; you're experiencing the future of freelancing.

AUTHENTIC JOBS: FINDING YOUR DREAM FREELANCE JOB

Embark on a journey to discover your dream freelance opportunities with Authentic Jobs. Uncover a platform that aligns your passions with projects, and learn how to craft applications that resonate with employers while authentically showcasing your unique self.

Authentic Jobs isn't just a platform; it's a gateway to finding freelance roles that speak to your passions and aspirations. Whether you're a designer, developer, writer, or possess any other skill, Authentic Jobs offers a curated selection of opportunities that resonate with your expertise.

Crafting applications that resonate with employers on Authentic Jobs involves more than just showcasing your skills; it's about presenting your genuine self. By aligning your application with the company's values, culture, and the unique skills you bring, you increase your chances of standing out and securing roles that align with your vision.

Here's how you can excel on Authentic Jobs:

- Research and Align: Understand the company's mission, values, and culture to tailor your application to their specific needs.
- Highlight Your Authenticity: Showcase your skills and experiences in a way that reflects your genuine passion for the industry.
- Craft Custom Applications: Tailor your applications for each role, addressing how your skills align with the project's requirements.
- Showcase Your Portfolio: Display your best work to demonstrate your capabilities and provide visual evidence of your expertise.
- Engage with Authenticity: Engage with potential employers and clients in a way that reflects your personality and professional approach.

Authentic Jobs is a platform where your passion meets purpose. As you navigate through opportunities, connect with potential clients, and craft applications that reflect your authentic self, you're not just job hunting; you're embarking on a journey to find meaningful roles that align with your aspirations.

TASKRABBIT: EMPOWERING LOCALIZED FREELANCING

Experience the power of localized freelancing with TaskRabbit. Uncover a platform that enables you to offer in-person services and build a reputation as a reliable and trusted local freelancer.

TaskRabbit isn't just a platform; it's a doorway to opportunities within your local community. Whether you're skilled in handyman tasks, cleaning, delivery, or any other service, TaskRabbit connects you with individuals in need of assistance, right in your neighborhood.

Providing in-person services on TaskRabbit goes beyond just completing tasks; it's about building relationships, establishing a local presence, and gaining the trust of your neighbors. By consistently delivering top-notch services, you can create a reputation as a reliable and capable local freelancer.

Here's how you can excel on TaskRabbit:

- Highlight Your Skills: Showcase your expertise and skills in your profile to attract clients seeking your specific services.
- Offer Competitive Pricing: Determine rates that reflect the local market while remaining appealing to potential clients.
- Build Strong Client Relationships: Prioritize clear communication, punctuality, and excellent service to foster positive client relationships.
- Provide Value: Go the extra mile to exceed client expectations, ensuring satisfaction and potential referrals.
- Promote Your Local Presence: Emphasize your commitment to serving your local community, building trust among potential clients.

TaskRabbit empowers you to tap into the needs of your community and offer valuable services that enhance the lives of others. As you navigate through tasks, engage with clients, and establish yourself as a reliable local freelancer, you're not just providing services; you're contributing to the well-being of your community.

FLEXJOBS: YOUR SOURCE FOR REMOTE AND FLEXIBLE JOBS

Uncover a world of remote and flexible opportunities with FlexJobs. Navigate a platform that connects you with remote work options and flexible arrangements. Learn how to create a standout profile that captures the attention of employers seeking versatile freelancers like you.

FlexJobs isn't just another job board; it's a specialized platform that curates a range of remote and flexible jobs. Whether you're looking for full-time remote positions or freelance gigs with adaptable hours, FlexJobs offers a diverse array of opportunities that cater to your preferences.

Crafting a standout profile on FlexJobs is essential to attract employers seeking freelancers who can adapt to various work styles and schedules. By highlighting your skills, experience, and your ability to thrive in remote and flexible roles, you position yourself as an ideal candidate for the evolving world of work.

Here's how you can excel on FlexJobs:

- Customize Your Profile: Tailor your profile to showcase your remote work experience, adaptability, and proficiency in virtual collaboration tools.
- Highlight Your Skills: Emphasize skills that demonstrate your ability to excel in remote or flexible roles, such as time management and communication.
- Optimize Your Search: Use filters and keywords to find opportunities that align with your desired work style and expertise.

- Craft Persuasive Applications: Tailor your applications to demonstrate your understanding of remote work dynamics and your commitment to delivering results.
- Engage Actively: Participate in discussions, webinars, and resources to enhance your understanding of remote work best practices.

FlexJobs empowers you to explore job opportunities that provide the flexibility you seek without compromising on your professional growth. As you navigate through remote and flexible jobs, connect with potential employers, and create a compelling profile, you're not just job hunting; you're embracing the evolving landscape of work.

SOLIDGIGS: CURATED FREELANCE SUCCESS

Embark on a journey of curated freelance success with SolidGigs. Explore a platform that offers pre-vetted projects, saving you time and providing access to high-quality freelance opportunities.

SolidGigs isn't just a platform; it's a solution that streamlines your freelancing journey. Instead of sifting through endless job listings, SolidGigs presents you with a selection of curated freelance projects that have been thoroughly vetted. This approach ensures that you spend less time searching and more time focusing on what you do best – delivering exceptional work.

Navigating through SolidGigs means accessing a pool of opportunities that align with your skills and preferences. By exploring these pre-screened gigs, you can confidently bid on projects knowing that they meet certain quality standards and have the potential to contribute to your professional growth.

Here's how SolidGigs enhances your freelancing experience:

- Time Savings: Spend less time searching for gigs and more time working on projects that resonate with your expertise.
- Quality Assurance: Engage with projects that have been curated to ensure their legitimacy, value, and potential for success.
- Tailored Recommendations: Receive personalized recommendations based on your skills, preferences, and desired working arrangements.
- Efficient Bidding: Craft tailored proposals for curated projects, focusing on showcasing your skills and value.
- Professional Growth: Engage with high-quality clients and projects that contribute to your portfolio and reputation.

SolidGigs empowers you to find freelancing success without the overwhelm. As you navigate through curated projects, engage with potential clients, and deliver exceptional work, you're not just freelancing; you're setting the stage for a fulfilling and prosperous freelance career.

1. Indeed (www.indeed.co.uk):

Indeed is one of the largest job search engines in the world. It aggregates job listings from various sources, including company websites and other job boards. You can search for jobs by location, industry, salary, and more.

2. Reed (www.reed.co.uk):

Reed is a well-known UK job portal offering a vast range of job opportunities. It allows you to upload your CV, set up job alerts, and apply directly to employers.

3. LinkedIn (www.linkedin.com/jobs):

LinkedIn is a professional networking platform that also hosts a robust job board. It offers a wide array of job postings and allows you to network with professionals in your field.

4. Totaljobs (www.totaljobs.com):

Totaljobs is a popular job board in the UK, providing access to thousands of job listings across various industries and sectors. It offers a user-friendly interface and personalized job alerts.

5. Monster (www.monster.co.uk):

Monster is a global job portal that caters to the UK job market as well. It provides job listings, career advice, and resources for job seekers. You can create a profile and upload your CV to apply for positions.

6. CV-Library (www.cv-library.co.uk):

CV-Library is a UK-based job board that allows job seekers to upload their CVs and search for jobs across multiple industries. It provides tools for creating and editing your CV.

7. Jobsite (www.jobsite.co.uk):

Jobsite is a comprehensive job portal with thousands of job listings across various sectors. It offers job alerts, CV database access, and resources to aid in your job search.

8. Guardian Jobs (jobs.theguardian.com):

The Guardian Jobs is an esteemed platform that features job listings from reputable employers. It covers a wide range of sectors and provides valuable career advice.

9. Gumtree (www.gumtree.com):

Gumtree is a classifieds website that also features job listings. It offers a range of opportunities, including part-time and freelance work.

10. CWJobs (www.cwjobs.co.uk):

CWJobs specializes in IT and tech job listings in the UK. It caters to professionals seeking roles in software development, cyber security, project management, and more.

11. Glassdoor (www.glassdoor.co.uk):

Glassdoor provides job listings, company reviews, and salary information. It helps job seekers gain insights into company culture and interview experiences.

12. Jobs.ac.uk (www.jobs.ac.uk):

Jobs.ac.uk focuses on academic and research positions in the UK. It offers opportunities in higher education institutions, research organizations, and related sectors.

13. Workinstartups.com (www.workinstartups.com):

Workinstartups.com is dedicated to job listings in startup companies. It offers a platform for job seekers looking to work in a dynamic and innovative environment.

14. Joblift (www.joblift.co.uk):

Joblift aggregates job postings from various sources and provides a user-friendly search experience. It covers a broad range of industries and sectors.

15. Fish4Jobs (www.fish4.co.uk):

Fish4Jobs features a wide range of job opportunities across different sectors. It offers job alerts and resources to enhance your job search.

16. JobsNHS (www.jobs.nhs.uk):

JobsNHS is the official job board for the National Health Service (NHS) in the UK. It lists job opportunities in healthcare, including nursing, medical, and administrative roles.

17. eFinancialCareers (www.efinancialcareers.co.uk):

eFinancialCareers focuses on job listings in the financial services sector, including banking, investment, and insurance. It caters to professionals at all career levels.

18. UK Staff Search (www.ukstaffsearch.com):

UK Staff Search provides a platform for job seekers and employers to connect across various industries. It offers a range of job listings and career resources.

19. JobisJob (www.jobisjob.co.uk):

JobisJob aggregates job listings from multiple sources and offers an intuitive search interface. It provides job alerts and the option to upload your CV.

20. CharityJob (www.charityjob.co.uk):

CharityJob is a dedicated job board for the nonprofit sector. It features job opportunities in charities, NGOs, and social enterprises, making it an ideal platform for those looking to make a positive impact.

21. The Dots (the-dots.com/jobs):

The Dots is a creative networking platform that also offers job listings in the creative industries. It connects professionals in design, advertising, marketing, and other creative fields.

22. Milkround (www.milkround.com):

Milkround specializes in graduate job opportunities in the UK. It caters to recent graduates and offers internships, graduate schemes, and entry-level positions.

23. BritishJobs (www.britishjobs.net):

BritishJobs provides a wide range of job listings across different industries and sectors. It allows job seekers to search by location, industry, and job type.

24. RetailChoice (www.retailchoice.com):

RetailChoice focuses on job opportunities in the retail industry. It offers positions in various retail sectors, including fashion, hospitality, and customer service.

25.   Adzuna (www.adzuna.co.uk):

Adzuna is a comprehensive job search engine that aggregates job listings from various sources. It provides salary estimates, company insights, and other helpful features.

26.   StudentJob UK (www.studentjob.co.uk):

StudentJob UK is designed for students and young professionals seeking part-time, seasonal, or temporary job opportunities. It offers flexible work options to fit around studies.

27.   TechNation Jobs (jobs.thetechnation.com):

TechNation Jobs is dedicated to job opportunities in the UK's tech industry. It covers positions in tech startups, scale-ups, and established tech companies.

28.   Law Society Gazette (jobs.lawgazette.co.uk):

Law Society Gazette features job listings specifically in the legal sector. It caters to lawyers, legal professionals, and law students looking for legal roles.

29.   Engineering Jobs (www.engineeringjobs.co.uk):

Engineering Jobs is a specialized job board focusing on engineering positions across different disciplines. It covers sectors such as civil engineering, mechanical engineering, and electrical engineering.

30. Hired (hired.com):

Hired is a platform that connects job seekers in the tech industry with top employers. It offers a curated job matching service and personalized support throughout the hiring process.

31. Guardian Careers (jobs.theguardian.com/careers):

Guardian Careers provides job listings and career resources across various industries. It features opportunities from reputable employers and offers insightful articles on career development.

32. Construction Jobs (www.constructionjobs.co.uk):

Construction Jobs is a job board dedicated to the construction industry. It offers a wide range of job opportunities, including construction management, architecture, and trades.

33. Charity People (www.charitypeople.co.uk):

Charity People specialize in job listings for the nonprofit sector. It focuses on positions in fundraising, marketing, communications, and charity management.

34. SecsInTheCity (www.secsinthecity.co.uk):

SecsInTheCity is a job portal for administrative and secretarial roles in the UK. It caters to professionals seeking positions in office administration, PA roles, and executive support.

35. Media Match (www.media-match.com):

Media Match is a job board specifically for the media and entertainment industry. It features job opportunities in film, television, advertising, journalism, and more.

36. All Cruise Jobs (www.allcruisejobs.com):

All Cruise Jobs is a dedicated job board for the cruise industry. It offers opportunities in various roles on cruise ships, including hospitality, entertainment, and marine positions.

37. Graduate Jobs (www.graduate-jobs.com):

Graduate Jobs is a platform specializing in entry-level positions for recent graduates. It features internships, graduate schemes, and trainee roles across different industries.

38. Aviation Job Search (www.aviationjobsearch.com):

Aviation Job Search caters to job seekers in the aviation industry. It features job opportunities in pilot, cabin crew, engineering, and airport operations roles.

39. Creativepool (www.creativepool.com):

Creativepool is a platform that connects creative professionals with job opportunities in the creative industries. It covers fields such as design, advertising, marketing, and digital media.

40.   Jooble (www.jooble.org.uk):

Jooble is a job search engine that aggregates listings from various sources. It provides a simple interface to search for jobs across multiple industries and locations.

41.   Jobserve (www.jobserve.com):

Jobserve focuses on IT and engineering job opportunities in the UK. It features positions in software development, network engineering, project management, and more.

42.   AllAboutCareers (www.allaboutcareers.com):

AllAboutCareers provides resources and job listings for students and graduates looking to pursue careers in various industries, including finance, law, marketing, and more.

43.   Jobsgopublic (www.jobsgopublic.com):

Jobsgopublic specializes in job opportunities within the public sector. It features positions in local government, healthcare, education, housing, and other public service areas.

44.   IT Jobs Watch (www.itjobswatch.co.uk):

IT Jobs Watch provides insights into the UK IT job market. It offers job listings, salary data, and trends in the IT industry to help job seekers make informed decisions.

45. RetailChoice (www.retailchoice.com):

RetailChoice focuses on job opportunities in the retail industry. It offers positions in various retail sectors, including fashion, hospitality, and customer service.

46. Caterer.com (www.caterer.com):

Caterer.com specializes in job listings in the hospitality and catering industry. It features positions in hotels, restaurants, event management, and related sectors.

47. JustEngineers (www.justengineers.net):

JustEngineers focuses on engineering job opportunities in the UK. It covers a wide range of engineering disciplines, including mechanical, electrical, civil, and aerospace..

48. Public Sector Jobs (www.publicsectorjobs.org.uk):

Public Sector Jobs is a job board that features job opportunities across different public sector organizations in the UK. It includes positions in local government, healthcare, and education.

49. Travelweekly Jobs (www.travelweekly.co.uk/jobs):

Travelweekly Jobs focuses on job opportunities in the travel and tourism industry. It features positions in travel agencies, airlines, tour operators, and hospitality.

50. Bubble Jobs (www.bubble-jobs.co.uk):

Bubble Jobs focuses on digital job opportunities, including roles in digital marketing, web development, social media, and e-commerce.

Tips for Maximizing Your Job Search:

- Create a compelling CV: Tailor your CV to highlight your relevant skills, experiences, and achievements for each job application.

- Set up job alerts: Utilize the job alert features provided by these websites to receive notifications about new job postings that match your preferences.
- Network: Leverage professional networking platforms like LinkedIn to connect with industry professionals, join relevant groups, and stay updated on industry trends and job opportunities.
- Research companies: Before applying for a job, research the companies you're interested in to gain insights into their culture, values, and work environment.
- Prepare for interviews: Brush up on common interview questions, practice your responses, and research the company to make a positive impression during interviews.
- Stay organized: Keep track of the jobs you have applied for, interview dates, and follow-up actions to ensure you stay organized throughout the job search process.

THE ART OF IMPRESSIVE RESUMES

Our resume serves as your initial introduction to potential employers. Learn how to craft a resume that not only highlights your skills and experience but also captures the essence of your professional journey. In this chapter, we delve into:

- Structuring your resume for maximum impact.
- Showcasing your accomplishments effectively.
- Utilizing keywords to pass through automated screening.
- Tailoring your resume for different job applications.

CRAFTING A COMPELLING PERSONAL BRAND

Your interview success starts before you even step into the interview room. Discover the importance of building a personal brand that sets you apart from the competition. This chapter covers:

- Identifying your unique strengths and qualities.
- Incorporating your personal brand into your resume.
- Creating a captivating professional summary.
- Showcasing your career progression and growth.

CHAPTER 3: PREPARING FOR INTERVIEW EXCELLENCE

Effective interview preparation is the cornerstone of a successful interview. Learn how to research the company, anticipate questions, and build confidence for the big day. In this chapter, we explore:

- Researching the company's mission, values, and culture.
- Practicing common interview questions and crafting impactful answers.
- Developing your own set of thoughtful questions to ask the interviewer.
- Techniques to manage interview anxiety and boost your confidence.

MASTERING NONVERBAL COMMUNICATION

Communication extends beyond words – your body language, gestures, and demeanor speak volumes. Discover the secrets of nonverbal communication that convey professionalism and confidence. This chapter discusses:

- Maintaining eye contact and a firm handshake.
- Utilizing positive body language to convey engagement.
- Navigating virtual interviews with grace and authenticity.
- Mirroring the tone and energy of the interviewer.

NAVIGATING CHALLENGING SCENARIOS

Interviews can sometimes present unexpected challenges. This chapter provides you with strategies to handle tricky questions, address employment gaps, and leave a lasting positive impression. Topics covered include:

- Addressing gaps in your employment history with honesty.
- Turning weaknesses into areas of growth and improvement.
- Providing examples of overcoming challenges in previous roles.
- Demonstrating adaptability and a willingness to learn.

THE FOLLOW-UP: SEALING THE DEAL

The interview doesn't end when you leave the room or sign off from the virtual call. Learn the significance of post-interview follow-up and how to leave a memorable impression. This chapter covers:

- Sending personalized thank-you notes and emails.
- Reiterating your interest in the position and the company.
- Emphasizing your alignment with the company's values and goals.
- Reflecting professionalism and gratitude throughout the process.

PAVING YOUR PATH TO INTERNATIONAL EMPLOYMENT

DEFINING YOUR GOALS AND PRIORITIES

Before embarking on your worldwide job search, reflect on your career aspirations, personal preferences, and long-term goals. Understanding what you seek in a job and its location will help you narrow down your options and make informed decisions.

RESEARCHING GLOBAL INDUSTRIES AND TRENDS

Different countries have unique strengths and industries. Delve into global economic trends and identify sectors that align with your skills and expertise. This proactive approach will enable you to target countries with flourishing job markets in your field.

CRAFTING AN INTERNATIONAL-FRIENDLY RESUME

TAILORING YOUR RESUME FOR GLOBAL IMPACT

Adapt your resume to cater to international employers. Highlight transferable skills, relevant experiences, and any cross-cultural exposure you may have had. Emphasize your adaptability and openness to diverse work environments.

SHOWCASING LANGUAGE PROFICIENCY

In an increasingly interconnected world, linguistic prowess holds immense value. Highlight your language proficiency, providing evidence of your ability to communicate effectively in a multicultural workplace.

NAVIGATING JOB SEARCH PLATFORMS AND RESOURCES

LEVERAGING ONLINE JOB PORTALS

Explore global job search platforms that cater to a diverse range of industries. Websites such as LinkedIn, Indeed, and Glassdoor offer filters to narrow your search based on location, job type, and experience level.

TAPPING INTO INTERNATIONAL NETWORKING

Networking transcends borders. Attend global networking events, workshops, and webinars to connect with professionals from various countries. Building a network can lead to invaluable insights and potential job referrals.

THE ART OF CRAFTING A COMPELLING APPLICATION

WRITING STELLAR COVER LETTERS

Craft personalized cover letters for each application, highlighting your enthusiasm for the role and your alignment with the company's values. Address the specific needs of the employer and demonstrate how you can contribute to their success.

ACE THE VIRTUAL INTERVIEW

As remote interviews become the norm, prepare diligently for virtual interactions. Test your technology beforehand, dress professionally, and ensure you're in a distraction-free environment. Make eye contact, articulate your responses clearly, and showcase your cultural sensitivity.

NAVIGATING VISAS AND IMMIGRATION

UNDERSTANDING VISA REQUIREMENTS

Each country has its own visa regulations for foreign workers. Research the visa requirements for your chosen destination, and ensure you meet the eligibility criteria before applying for jobs.

SEEKING LEGAL ASSISTANCE

Navigating the complexities of international work permits can be challenging. Consult with legal experts or immigration consultants to ensure a smooth transition and compliance with local laws.

The Fundamentals of Passive Income

Passive income, the holy grail of financial independence, is income that is earned with minimal to no effort on your part once the initial setup is complete. It allows you to break free from the constraints of traditional employment and grants you the freedom to live life on your terms. While it may seem like a dream reserved for the lucky few, the truth is that anyone can achieve passive income with the right knowledge and strategies.

To embark on this journey, it is crucial to understand the difference between passive income and active income. Active income is earned through direct effort and exchange of time for money. It includes salaries, wages, and commissions, where your income is directly proportional to the hours you work. On the other hand, passive income is generated from assets that work for you, even when you're not actively involved.

One of the key principles underlying passive income is the concept of leverage. By leveraging your time, money, and resources, you can create income streams that continue to generate revenue long after the initial investment. For example, investing in rental properties allows you to earn monthly rental income while benefiting from the potential appreciation of the property's value over time.

Another essential aspect of passive income is scalability. Unlike active income, which is limited by the number of hours you can work in a day, passive income has the potential to scale exponentially. By leveraging systems, automation, and technology, you can multiply your income streams without a linear increase in effort.

Building your passive income mindset

We laid the foundation by understanding the fundamentals of passive income. Now, in Chapter 2, we will delve into the mindset required to build a solid foundation for your passive income endeavors. Developing the right mindset is crucial for long-term success in generating passive income streams.

❖ **EMBRACE A WEALTH MINDSET:**

To embark on your passive income journey, it's essential to adopt a wealth mindset. This mindset focuses on abundance, opportunities, and the belief that there is enough wealth to go around for everyone. Instead of a scarcity mindset, where you believe that resources are limited, cultivate an abundance mindset that opens your mind to new possibilities and income-generating ideas.

❖ **SET CLEAR GOALS:**

Goal setting is a critical aspect of building your passive income empire. Clearly define your financial goals, both short-term and long-term. Your goals will serve as your roadmap, keeping you focused and motivated along the way. Write down your goals and review them regularly to track your progress and make any necessary adjustments.

❖ DEVELOP PATIENCE AND PERSISTENCE:

Generating passive income takes time and effort. It's important to have patience and understand that results may not come overnight. Be prepared for setbacks and challenges along the way. Persistence is key when it comes to building passive income streams. Stay committed to your goals and keep pushing forward, even when faced with obstacles.

❖ EMBRACE CONTINUOUS LEARNING:

The world of passive income is constantly evolving. To stay ahead of the curve, embrace continuous learning. Read books, attend seminars, listen to podcasts, and follow industry experts to expand your knowledge and gain insights into new opportunities. The more you learn, the better equipped you'll be to make informed decisions and take advantage of emerging trends.

❖ DEVELOP MULTIPLE STREAMS OF PASSIVE INCOME:

Diversification is crucial in the world of passive income. Relying on a single income stream can be risky. Aim to develop multiple streams of passive income to safeguard against potential losses and create a more stable financial foundation. Explore different avenues such as real estate, stock investments, online businesses, and royalties from intellectual property.

❖ CULTIVATE A POSITIVE MINDSET:

A positive mindset is essential for success in any endeavor. Surround yourself with positivity and eliminate negative influences from your life. Practice gratitude and visualization techniques to reinforce positive thinking. By cultivating a positive mindset, you'll attract more opportunities and overcome challenges with resilience.

❖ LEVERAGE AUTOMATION AND SYSTEMS:

One of the key advantages of passive income is the ability to automate income-generating processes. Embrace technology and leverage automation tools and systems to streamline your passive income streams. Whether it's automating your online business or using property management services for rental properties, find ways to reduce your active involvement and maximize your passive income potential.

❖ NETWORK AND COLLABORATE:

Networking and collaboration can open doors to new opportunities and valuable connections. Engage with like-minded individuals, join relevant communities, and attend networking events. Collaborate with others who share similar goals and interests. By building a network of supportive individuals, you can leverage their knowledge, experiences, and resources to accelerate your passive income journey.

By adopting these mindset principles, you'll be well on your way to building a solid foundation for generating passive income. Remember, building passive income streams is a journey, and success comes from a combination of mindset, knowledge, and consistent action. Stay focused, be patient, and embrace the possibilities that passive income can bring into your life.

Exploring Real Estate Investments for Passive Income

Real estate has long been considered a lucrative avenue for wealth creation and can provide a steady stream of passive income if approached strategically.

❖ **UNDERSTANDING REAL ESTATE INVESTMENT OPTIONS:**

Before diving into real estate investments, it's crucial to understand the various options available. You can choose to invest in residential properties, commercial properties, vacation rentals, or even real estate investment trusts (REITs). Each option comes with its own set of advantages, risks, and potential returns. Take the time to research and evaluate which type of real estate investment aligns best with your financial goals and risk tolerance.

❖ **CONDUCTING THOROUGH MARKET RESEARCH:**

Market research is a fundamental step in any real estate investment venture. Familiarize yourself with the local real estate market and identify areas with potential for growth and demand. Look for neighborhoods or cities experiencing economic development, job growth, and population increases. Additionally, consider factors like property taxes, rental demand, and the overall investment climate. A comprehensive understanding of the market will help you make informed decisions and maximize your passive income potential.

❖ ANALYZING INVESTMENT PROPERTIES:

When evaluating potential investment properties, conduct thorough financial analysis. Consider factors such as purchase price, rental income potential, expenses (including property taxes, insurance, maintenance, and property management fees), and projected appreciation. Calculate the cash flow, return on investment (ROI), and cap rate to assess the profitability of the property. It's essential to perform due diligence and work with real estate professionals if needed to ensure accurate analysis.

❖ FINANCING YOUR REAL ESTATE INVESTMENTS:

Financing plays a significant role in real estate investments, especially for those starting with limited capital. Explore different financing options such as mortgages, partnerships, private lenders, or real estate crowd funding platforms. Evaluate the terms, interest rates, and repayment structures to determine the most suitable financing method for your investment goals.

❖ ENGAGING PROFESSIONAL SERVICES:

Real estate investments can involve complex legal, financial, and management aspects. It's advisable to engage professional services to ensure a smooth and successful investment journey. Seek the expertise of real estate agents, attorneys, property managers, and accountants to guide you through the process. Their knowledge and experience can help you navigate legal requirements, find suitable properties, handle tenant relations, and optimize your investment returns.

❖ IMPLEMENTING PROPERTY MANAGEMENT STRATEGIES:

Efficient property management is crucial for passive income generation in real estate. Whether you choose to self-manage or hire a property management company, establish robust systems and processes to streamline operations. Ensure regular property maintenance, prompt rent collection, and effective tenant screening to minimize vacancies and maximize rental income. A well-managed property not only enhances your passive income but also contributes to long-term appreciation and tenant satisfaction.

❖ SCALING YOUR REAL ESTATE PORTFOLIO:

Once you've successfully established one or more passive income streams through real estate, consider scaling your portfolio. As you gain experience and confidence, explore opportunities to acquire additional properties or diversify your real estate investments. Scaling allows you to amplify your passive income potential and build wealth over time. However, always approach scaling strategically, considering your financial capacity, market conditions, and risk management strategies.

❖ **STAYING UPDATED AND ADAPTING:**

The real estate market is dynamic and subject to changing trends, regulations, and economic conditions. Stay updated with industry news, market trends, and legal developments that may impact your investments. Be adaptable and willing to adjust your strategies as needed. Continuously educate yourself through real estate seminars, workshops, and networking events to stay ahead of the curve and maximize your passive income opportunities.

Real estate investments offer a powerful pathway to generating passive income and building long-term wealth. By understanding the market, analyzing properties diligently, leveraging financing options, and implementing effective property management strategies, you can unlock the potential of real estate as a passive income stream.

Generating Passive Income through Dividend Investing

Dividend investing involves investing in stocks and funds that pay regular dividends, allowing investors to earn passive income while benefiting from the potential growth of their investments.

❖ **UNDERSTANDING DIVIDEND INVESTING:**

Dividends are payments made by companies to their shareholders as a portion of the company's profits. Dividend investing involves selecting stocks or funds that have a track record of consistently paying dividends. These dividends can provide a reliable stream of passive income, allowing investors to earn money even without selling their shares.

❖ **IDENTIFYING DIVIDEND-PAYING STOCKS:**

When engaging in dividend investing, it's important to identify stocks with a history of consistent dividend payments. Look for companies with a strong financial track record, stable earnings, and a commitment to returning profits to shareholders. Dividend-paying stocks are often found in sectors such as utilities, consumer goods, healthcare, and telecommunications. Conduct thorough research and analyze financial data to assess the sustainability and growth potential of dividends.

❖ **DIVERSIFYING YOUR DIVIDEND PORTFOLIO:**

As with any investment strategy, diversification is key in dividend investing. Building a diversified portfolio helps reduce risk and increase the potential for stable passive income. Invest in companies across different sectors and sizes to spread out the risk.

Additionally, consider diversifying your investments by including dividend-focused funds or exchange-traded funds (ETFs) that hold a basket of dividend-paying stocks.

❖ ASSESSING DIVIDEND METRICS:

When evaluating dividend-paying stocks, it's important to consider various dividend metrics. Key metrics include dividend yield, dividend growth rate, and payout ratio. The dividend yield indicates the annual dividend payment as a percentage of the stock price. The dividend growth rate measures the historical increase in dividends over time. The payout ratio represents the proportion of a company's earnings paid out as dividends. A careful analysis of these metrics can help you identify stocks with sustainable and growing dividends.

❖ REINVESTING DIVIDENDS:

One of the most powerful aspects of dividend investing is the ability to reinvest dividends. Many companies offer dividend reinvestment plans (DRIPs) that allow you to automatically reinvest dividends back into purchasing more shares. By reinvesting dividends, you can take advantage of compounding returns, where your dividend income generates additional shares, further increasing your passive income potential over time.

❖ EVALUATING TAX IMPLICATIONS:

Dividend income is subject to taxation. It's important to understand the tax implications of dividend investing in your specific jurisdiction. Different countries may have varying tax rates and rules regarding dividend taxation. Consult with a tax professional to determine the most tax-efficient strategies for dividend investing, such as utilizing tax-advantaged accounts like Individual Retirement Accounts (IRAs) or Tax-Free Savings Accounts (TFSAs).

❖ STAYING INFORMED AND MONITORING INVESTMENTS:

Successful dividend investing requires staying informed and monitoring your investments regularly. Keep track of the performance and financial health of the companies in your portfolio. Stay updated on company news, earnings reports, and dividend announcements. Regularly review your portfolio's composition and make adjustments as needed to ensure alignment with your investment goals and risk tolerance.

❖ LONG-TERM PERSPECTIVE AND PATIENCE:

Dividend investing is a long-term strategy that requires patience and a focus on the bigger picture. While dividend income can provide passive income in the short term, the true power of dividend investing lies in its compounding effect over time. By reinvesting dividends and allowing your investments to grow, you can potentially generate substantial passive income and build long-term wealth.

Dividend investing offers the potential for both income and growth, making it an attractive avenue for passive income generation. By understanding dividend metrics, diversifying your portfolio, reinvesting dividends, and staying informed, you can create a stream of passive income that grows steadily over time.

Creating Passive Income with Digital Products and Online Courses

We explored the power of dividend investing for generating passive income. Now, in Chapter 5, we will dive into the world of digital products and online courses as a means of creating passive income streams. With the rise of the internet and digital platforms, individuals have the opportunity to leverage their knowledge and expertise to create and sell digital products and online courses to a global audience.

❖ IDENTIFYING YOUR EXPERTISE AND PASSION:

To create successful digital products and online courses, start by identifying your expertise and passion. Consider your skills, knowledge, and experiences that can add value to others. Are you an expert in a specific field? Do you have specialized knowledge that can help solve problems or fulfill a need? Identifying your niche will not only make your products more targeted but also fuel your passion and motivation.

❖ RESEARCHING MARKET DEMAND:

Once you've identified your expertise, it's important to research the market demand for your chosen niche. Are there people actively seeking information or solutions in your area of expertise? Use keyword research tools, conduct surveys, and engage with your target audience to gauge their needs and interests. Understanding the market demand will help you create digital products and courses that resonate with your audience and have a higher chance of success.

❖ CREATING DIGITAL PRODUCTS:

Digital products come in various forms, such as e-books, audio files, templates, software, and multimedia content. Choose a format that aligns with your expertise and the preferences of your target audience. For example, if you're a writer, you might create e-books on specialized topics. If you're a graphic designer, you could create customizable templates or graphics. Focus on providing valuable and actionable content that solves a problem or fulfills a need.

❖ DEVELOPING ONLINE COURSES:

Online courses offer a structured learning experience and can be highly profitable as a passive income stream. Outline the learning objectives, modules, and lessons of your course. Create engaging video content, written materials, quizzes, and assignments to enhance the learning experience. Leverage technology platforms and learning management systems to host and deliver your course to students worldwide.

❖ BUILDING A SALES FUNNEL:

To effectively sell your digital products and online courses, it's essential to build a sales funnel. A sales funnel is a step-by-step process that guides potential customers from awareness to purchase. Start by attracting your target audience through content marketing, social media, and search engine optimization. Offer free valuable content or lead magnets to capture email addresses and build a subscriber list. Nurture your subscribers with valuable information and gradually introduce your paid products or courses.

❖ LEVERAGING PLATFORMS AND MARKETPLACES:

While you can host your digital products and online courses on your own website or platform, consider leveraging existing platforms and marketplaces to reach a wider audience. Platforms like Amazon Kindle Direct Publishing, Udemy, Teachable, and

Shopify offer built-in audiences and marketing tools. Research and select platforms that align with your product or course type, target audience, and revenue-sharing model

❖ AUTOMATING SALES AND DELIVERY:

One of the key advantages of digital products and online courses is the ability to automate sales and delivery. Implement systems and tools that allow for seamless purchasing, payment processing, and content delivery. Utilize email automation to deliver welcome messages, course materials, and upsell offers. By automating these processes, you can generate passive income without the need for continuous manual intervention.

❖ PROVIDING ONGOING SUPPORT AND UPDATES:

Creating passive income through digital products and online courses doesn't end with the initial launch. Provide ongoing support to your customers or students to ensure their satisfaction and encourage positive reviews and referrals. Regularly update your products and courses to stay relevant and address changes in your field. By maintaining a strong relationship with your audience and delivering value consistently, you can generate a steady stream of passive income over the long term.

Mastering affiliate marketing for passive income streams

Affiliate marketing allows individuals to promote products or services and earn commissions for every sale made through their referral. It's a powerful strategy that can generate passive income when executed effectively.

❖ UNDERSTANDING AFFILIATE MARKETING:

Affiliate marketing is a performance-based marketing model where affiliates earn commissions by promoting products or services. Affiliates partner with companies or brands and receive a unique affiliate link or coupon code. When someone makes a purchase using that link or code, the affiliate earns a percentage of the sale. It's a win-win scenario, benefiting both the affiliate and the company.

❖ SELECTING PROFITABLE AFFILIATE PROGRAMS:

To succeed in affiliate marketing, it's crucial to choose profitable affiliate programs that align with your target audience and niche. Research and evaluate potential affiliate programs based on factors such as commission rates, cookie duration (the time period during which you can earn a commission for a referral), product quality, and reputation of the company. Look for programs that offer competitive commissions and provide valuable resources for affiliates.

❖ BUILDING A TRUSTWORTHY PLATFORM:

Building trust with your audience is paramount in affiliate marketing. Create a trustworthy platform such as a blog, website, or social media presence where you can share valuable content and recommendations. Focus on providing genuine and unbiased reviews of products or services that you promote. Transparency and honesty will foster trust, resulting in higher engagement and increased likelihood of conversions.

❖ CREATING COMPELLING CONTENT:

Content creation is at the core of successful affiliate marketing. Develop high-quality and compelling content that educates, entertains, and addresses the needs of your target audience. Write informative blog posts, create engaging videos, or record podcasts that highlight the benefits and features of the products or services you promote. Incorporate your affiliate links naturally within your content, making it seamless and non-intrusive.

❖ UTILIZING MULTIPLE PROMOTION CHANNELS:

Diversify your promotion channels to reach a wider audience and maximize your passive income potential. Leverage social media platforms, email marketing, paid advertising, and search engine optimization (SEO) strategies. Each channel has its own strengths and target audience, so choose the ones that align with your niche and provide the best reach and engagement.

❖ IMPLEMENTING EFFECTIVE CALL-TO-ACTIONS (CTAS):

A strong call-to-action (CTA) can significantly increase your conversion rates in affiliate marketing. Encourage your audience to take action by including clear and compelling CTAs within your content. Use persuasive language and emphasize the benefits or incentives associated with the product or service. Experiment with different CTAs, such as buttons, banners, or text links, to identify what works best for your audience.

❖ TRACKING AND ANALYZING PERFORMANCE:

Tracking and analyzing the performance of your affiliate marketing efforts is crucial to optimizing your strategy and maximizing your passive income. Utilize tracking tools and analytics to monitor the click-through rates, conversion rates, and overall performance of your affiliate links. Identify which products or promotions are generating the most revenue and focus on optimizing those. Continuously analyze and refine your approach based on the data to improve your results over time.

❖ CULTIVATING RELATIONSHIPS WITH AFFILIATE PARTNERS:

Building strong relationships with your affiliate partners can open doors to exclusive promotions, higher commissions, and additional resources. Communicate regularly with your affiliate managers or contacts, provide feedback and suggestions, and collaborate on promotional campaigns. Cultivating these relationships can lead to long-term partnerships that benefit both parties and increase your passive income potential.

Diversifying Your Passive Income Portfolio for Long-Term Success

Diversification involves spreading your investments across different asset classes and income streams to reduce risk, increase stability, and enhance long-term success.

❖ THE BENEFITS OF DIVERSIFICATION:

Diversification is a key strategy for building a robust passive income portfolio. By diversifying, you reduce the reliance on a single income source, minimizing the impact of any potential setbacks or fluctuations in one particular market or investment. Diversification allows you to spread your risk and capture the benefits of different income streams, increasing your chances of long-term success.

❖ EXPLORE DIFFERENT ASSET CLASSES:

Consider diversifying your passive income portfolio by exploring different asset classes. Look beyond a single type of investment, such as real estate or stocks, and consider other options. This may include bonds, mutual funds, index funds, peer-to-peer lending, royalties from intellectual property, or even investing in small businesses. Each asset class has its own risk and return characteristics, and diversifying across them can provide a more balanced portfolio.

❖ SEEK MULTIPLE PASSIVE INCOME STREAMS:

Within each asset class, aim to create multiple passive income streams, For example, if you invest in real estate; consider diversifying by owning different types of properties, such as residential, commercial, or vacation rentals. If you have digital products or online courses, explore additional avenues for monetization, such as affiliate marketing or licensing your content. By diversifying within each income stream, you further reduce risk and increase the stability of your overall portfolio.

❖ CONSIDER GEOGRAPHIC DIVERSIFICATION:

Geographic diversification is another aspect to consider. Invest in different regions or countries to reduce the impact of localized economic conditions or regulatory changes. Look for markets with stable growth, strong rental demand, and favorable investment climates. By spreading your investments across multiple geographic locations, you can mitigate risks associated with a single market and tap into various income opportunities.

❖ EVALUATE RISK AND RETURN PROFILES:

When diversifying your passive income portfolio, evaluate the risk and return profiles of each investment. Some income streams may have higher risk but potentially offer greater returns, while others may provide steady but lower returns. Assess your risk tolerance, investment goals, and time horizon to create a diversified portfolio that aligns with your objectives. Strive for a balance between conservative and growth-oriented investments.

❖ REGULARLY REVIEW AND REBALANCE:

Diversification is not a one-time action; it requires ongoing review and rebalancing. Regularly assess the performance of each income stream and make adjustments as needed. Monitor market conditions, industry trends, and economic factors that may impact your investments. Periodically rebalance your portfolio to ensure it remains aligned with your risk tolerance and investment objectives.

❖ EMBRACE INNOVATION AND EMERGING TRENDS:

Stay abreast of innovation and emerging trends in various industries. The world is constantly evolving, and new opportunities for passive income may arise. Keep an eye on technological advancements, changing consumer behaviors, and emerging markets. Be open to exploring new income streams or adapting existing ones to stay ahead of the curve and maximize your passive income potential.

❖ CONTINUOUSLY EDUCATE YOURSELF:

As you diversify your passive income portfolio, never stop learning. Stay informed about the different asset classes and income streams you're invested in. Educate yourself about new investment strategies, tax regulations, and market trends. Attend seminars, read books, and engage with experts in the fields you're exploring. Continuous learning empowers you to make informed decisions and adapt to changing circumstances.

Diversifying your passive income portfolio is a wise approach for long-term success. By exploring different asset classes, seeking multiple passive income streams, considering geographic diversification, evaluating risk and return profiles, regularly reviewing and rebalancing, embracing innovation, and continuously educating yourself, you can create a resilient and profitable portfolio that generates passive income and builds lasting wealth.

Remember, generating passive income requires dedication, persistence, and a long-term perspective. Stay committed to your goals, adapt to changing circumstances, and enjoy the journey as you unlock the true potential of passive income. May your endeavors be fruitful, and may your passive income streams pave the way to a fulfilling and prosperous future.

www.ingramcontent.com/pod-product-compliance
Lightning Source LLC
Chambersburg PA
CBHW050231230526
45470CB00005B/1904